Because I Knew

Because I Knew

Poetry
by
R. Ummi Modeste

Because I Knew is published by Muse City Press
musecitypress@gmail.com

First Edition: November 2020
Printed in the United States of America
ISBN: 9781953481009

DEDICATION

For my Moms: Midgie, Nettie and Glo, who also knew. For my Godmother Committee: Carrie, Elaine, Dorothy, Fran, Lida, Selvena and Shirley. For every woman who has ever mothered me, and in profound gratitude to Grace Beniquez, who mothered this book into existence.

Dear Reader,
I pray my words stir something in your spirit
Best,
[illegible]

TABLE OF CONTENTS

INTRODUCTION

This compilation of my poetry is more than just a random selection of writing; it is my soul represented in ink. Each piece poured out of me of its own volition, during times when I was feeling particularly pensive, angry, reflective, sassy, sexy or just grateful; truly, when I was just particularly FEELING. Some of these poems came forth as a way of writing myself out of an abyss created by grief, loss and heartache. I hope that reading them will enrich your life and encourage you to find a way to work through any situation that may be troubling you. I pray that you choose to celebrate the small joys that we all encounter every day because deep in your heart, you also know, we must hold onto those moments of joy to get us through the rough times.

R. Ummi Modeste
Jersey City, NJ

FOREWORD

R. Ummi Modeste has shared her soul and poured her heart out in this powerful compilation of poetry entitled, "Because I Knew". I met Ummi at Church Unusual, also known as St. Paul Community Baptist Church. We were soul sisters in the writing ministry, Dabar. I recall the writing prompts and thematic performances that initiated our desire to share honestly, authentically and powerfully. Dabar was the catalyst that jumpstarted the unveiling of our stories through the art of writing.

Ummi, along with our dear friends and brothers, Tracy Jackson and Keith "Just Sayin" Richards, branched out to create East Brooklyn Poets, a group of artists who shared life experiences and observations while offering commentary and healing through poetry and spoken word. Each presentation was a unique event where members of the audience were active participants. Open Mic followed every performance, offering everyone an opportunity to floss their lyrical skills and talents. Although they haven't performed together in a while, the surviving members (R. Ummi Modeste, Shahmet Gordon, Bruce "Loose Bruce" Booker, Robin St. Clair, Erwin E.A. Thomas and Grace Beniquez) are still very actively writing, sharing, healing, and teaching.

On a personal note, Ummi and I have nurtured and cared for each other's children. We are spiritual sisters and have endured much together. I am so excited for the manifestation of her literary work and even more excited to experience her growth and development throughout the years.

In her most vulnerable piece, "No Time For the Pain", Ummi reveals her deepest, darkest secrets and shares her intimate thoughts with authenticity and raw honesty. She tells a familiar story of masking her pain through smiles, stuffing the pain with food and experiences of unrequited love. In this book, Ummi takes us on a mental and emotional journey of her life. You will laugh, cry, feel and experience one woman's journey from self-inquiry to self affirmation.

Robin St. Clair
TheRiteStep
Brooklyn, NY

I AM

Ummi/Rhea/Rhee/Rhee-Rhee/Ummilah/Ma/Auntie...

I am the one who feels more deeply laughs louder and harder,

cries more easily and hurts too much

Aunt Rhea/Rhea Moe/Auntie Rhea/Auntie Ummi/Rhee-Moe/

Rhee-yah...

I am the one who angers quickly then laughs again

Ummi Moe/Baby Sis/Loisey/Daughter/Girl-child/MoMoe/

Wife...

I am the one who is a flash flame and a burning ember and

a cool lake and a crashing wave

Coach's sister/Lil'Sis/Sistah Ummi/Mrs. Hall

I am...

Gary's wife

I am...

Michael's sister-friend

I am...

Wendi's caregiver

I am...

all that I have ever been
A part of me will always be in Mommy's bedroom
921 Washington Avenue
with Gary on Chester Street
beneath the proscenium
in Safiya, Nia, Nahmir, Jelani
in a grave on Long Island
in the souls of two long dead children
A part of me will always be
lost lost lost gone
forever.

¿QUIÉN SOY YO?

¿Quién es ella? You ask aloud, sure that I won't understand.
¿Quién soy YO? I am the grandmother you don't acknowledge
la tía that you pretend doesn't exist
the one you no longer visit back home

¿Quién soy YO? I am your sister
who yearns to stay connected
the one whose heart breaks each time you turn away.

¿Quién soy YO?
I was your neighbor on S. Union or 174th Street
before you moved to Tower Hill or the Upper West Side
the one you ignore in Stop 'N Shop as you do your best
to smile and chat with Karen down the aisle

¿Quién soy YO? ¿QUIÉN SOY YO?
I am you.
The part of you that has NOT been bleached,

straightened and Anglicized into oblivion.

The part of you that doesn't
need to hablar Español loudly in public
to prove that you're not a part of ME.

¿Quién soy YO? I am your grandmother, your aunt, your sister, your neighbor who still loves you and will accept you once again when you learn to accept your Black self.

WHAT MOMMY SAID

Mommy raised me to be a proper lady.
She taught me to e-nun-ci-ate,
make eye contact,
give a firm handshake,
speak the King's English.

Mommy said remember that you represent
yourself,
your family,
and God
every time you leave this house;
don't bring any shame on the family name;
don't be common in the street.
Always carry yourself above the fray.
You are a descendant of royalty.

Mommy had me practice with the red Webster's
and then the green World Book on my head.

Five paces this way.
Five paces that way.
Other kids said I walked like I had a stick up my...
All rise for the Queen! they teased.

Ignore those street urchins, Mommy said
If you don't know who you are, no one else will.
You are a descendant of royalty.
You are meant to frequent the finest places.

When you walk down the street with your King,
Make him proud to have you on his arm.
Make other men envy him
And women wonder what spell you cast.

Have other people's children wish you were their mom
and have the whole neighborhood
look at you with admiration.
A refined lady with excellent upbringing,

that's what everyone should see, Mommy said.
Upon entering an elegant establishment,
she told me, you must wait
for your King to pull out your chair,
sit down gently,
cross your legs at the ankles,
place your napkin demurely in your lap,
blot the corners of your mouth delicately when necessary.
Chew with your mouth closed.
Swallow before speaking.
Maintain excellent manners and
remember, you descended from royalty.

But when you're at home, Mommy said
and it's just you and your King,
release your hair,
fix him a drink in his favorite glass
with just the right number of ice cubes,
and while he's enjoying it

prepare his meal with love and attention;
pour your affection into everything you offer him
and make sure that the special on the menu
is always
you.
Because when you feed your man well at home
he has no need for restaurants.

NO TIME TO FEEL THE PAIN

I need to cry
I've had tears caught in my spirit for weeks but I can't release them.
I needed to cry in New Orleans
People trying to return home with little or no assistance.
Children still smiling and eager to learn,
three addresses and two schools after The Storm.
One of those damn FEMA trailers could fit inside my house.
A whole family lives there?
Historical landmarks abandoned
William Frantz School hasn't been this empty since
Ruby Bridges enrolled.
Still-ghostly neighborhoods make me want to weep
But I can't release this ocean of tears dammed up
behind a smiling face and peaceful countenance.
Tears that gather at the brink of
my eyes, a pair of well-built levees
no hurricane waters can overcome

The Army Corps of Engineers should consult me.
Oh, but there's fun to be had by all in the Quarter.

I needed to cry when I went 0 for 3
with my grad school applications
Never experienced 100% rejection before.
Is my writing too Black for you?
Am I not mainstream enough?
Or is it just too sad to bear?

I needed to cry when he said, "I do", to her, not me.
Wearing my bleeding soul like a sexy sheath,
hiding again.
Who could see my anguish?

I needed to cry when you said, "I do", then you didn't.

"I haven't got time for the pain..."
Never acknowledged it

Never spoke the words aloud or declared the pain's existence.
Never poured it out,
instead poured poisons in to mask the pain,
bathed it in analgesics
stuffed it with appetizers
covered it in yards and yards of bright cloth
but never ever expressed it.
Too busy being responsible.
Too busy being a role model.
"What would Jesus do?"
I never looked at the pain up close
Never really felt it.
Never cried the tears of grief for
all the leaving
all the dying
all the not wanting me
all the bad choices and unmet needs
for the babies who didn't breathe
and the love that wasn't shared

and the lies, the lies
for the anniversaries that never happened
and the sorrowful ones that did
for the unanswered calls
and the empty arms
When was I supposed to cry?
When did I have time to grieve
the promises unfulfilled
the dreams deferred, dissolved, destroyed?
It just never seemed like the right time.
"I haven't got time for the pain..."

CAN'T STAY AWAY

As I lie across the softness of these rumpled,
still-damp sheets
from which you so recently arose,
I inhale to recapture your scent,
I bask in the heat your skin left behind,
remembering its smoothness against mine.
I thought today I'd tell you,
I have to stay away,
separate myself from the sweet nectar of your kisses
and the security of being wrapped in your strong arms.

Instead, I discovered that I barely need a blanket
when you're in this bed with me.
Every night, I used so many layers to shield me from the cold,
but with you as my quilt,
I was naked and warm.

Why did you share your poem with me?

Why did you expose your pain?
It disturbed me because I heard my own voice in it.
It disturbed me because it was about a situation
too similar to ours,
too familiar to you.
I want somehow to be different, special, new;
but I guess we're both too experienced for that.

Today I thought I'd tell you, it's time to be responsible,
live up to what's expected of us
deny our passion and
do what's right
Instead, I discovered another flavor on your skin;
I slept with the sound of your breath on my cheek and
the tickle of your mustache in my ear.

Today, your touch singed my skin and
burned a hole in my resolve.
You anointed me,

massaged me with almond scented oil and caressed me

as if I were your own.

And today, just for these precious moments, today, I am.

WHO NAMES ME?

Adunni calls me Mom-meeeee; I love the music in it.
I was Mommy before I ever gave birth.
My son TJ calls me Ma, thrilling me every time because
he is not a child of my womb,
but of my heart.
Nasir calls me Grammy,
My nephews put a whole lot of bass in Auntie Rhea.

You can name me if I let you,
call out my name if I make you...Say my name, say my name.
Modeste, Modesto, Modesté... Quién sabe?

I miss hearing Mommy say, "Hi Rhee-Rhee."

Prayer Intercessor/Warrior, that's me.
Sistah Girl...third Sis in We-3.
Spirit whisperers call out to me in my sleep,
naming me Girlchild, begging me,

"Tell our stories, speak our peace."
I hear the sun rising over Africa
When a Black or Brown man calls me Baby or Mami.

You can only call me by my gov'ment if I say so.
That's how I know how you know me.
Did you meet me in a Rhea situation
or are you down with Ummi?
Holla at me with the wrong name
you might be surprised who answers.
Rhea and Ummi inhabit the same temple, but you better pray
Ummi keeps Rhea in check.
Rhea was a Christian and a Muslim,
but it's Ummi who knows God.
Lord, be a sentry at the door of my mouth.

Mommy, Ummi, Loisey, Miss! I'll answer to all of them.
Coach Moe's sister, Adunni's Mom, Namaste Sis.
Yes, that will get my attention.

I'll even turn around if you say, "Wendi!"

Who names me?

I do.

My parents did.

God has.

You can name me only if you

love me and claim me as your own.

Yuu can name me if I let you

Call out my name if I make you...Say my name, say my name.

A POEM FOR MY LITTLE GIRL

Sweet, round face, fat cheeks
and the distinctive Kool-Aid,
all-teeth-showing-
eyes-disappearing
Modeste smile,
thick legs-miniatures of your mother's and auntie's,
and Girl, whatchu doin' with all them hips already?
You're only eight, my baby girl.

Dreadlocks flying/flapping up and down as you dance,
          jump double-dutch,
                    ride your bike into the wind fearlessly,
something Mommy never learned how to do.
I want you to have time to be a little girl.
To play with Baby Born and even Barbie,
and dress-up clothes,
creating your own shows in costumes worn only once,
left over from dance recitals where Daddy and I

pretended not to cry.
You're only eight, my baby girl.

Take time to play outside with your little girlfriends on the block,visit each other's houses-doing hair with fifty-thousand different color barrettes, bobos and scrunchies;
(Girl, stop leaving that mannequin lying around; she's spooky!)
painting each others' nails iridescent blue with a special design for the big toes.

I love the artistry of the flowers, butterflies and ying/yang
you apply to your play sisters' ankles, backs and bellies
in your tattoo parlor on the living room couch.

Adulthood will come soon enough and last a very long time.
You're only eight; enjoy being my little girl.
Love,
Mommy

NOW I AM MOMMY

I am the Mommy now.

I am the one who enforces the rules, endures the tantrums,

explains everything;

the one who longs for more time and money just for fun.

I am the "mean parent"

I am the one who fed you from my own body

kissed your every wound,

inhaled your scent

and recognized it as my own

I am Mommy now

the one who sometimes cries when your needs and wants

conflict with my own

A part of me wonders, "Am I good enough?"

I am Mommy

the one who has to arrange child care if I want a little time to

myself
to take a class
sit in silence, or
OMG!
go out?

A part of me resents Daddy's freedom
and his label as the "nice parent".
Yet all of me honors and respects him for choosing to be a good dad, your dad

I am Mommy
who wants to play more and scold less

Mommy:
chauffeur
breadwinner
peacemaker
cook

maid

laundress

beautician

official runner of all errands

teacher

Mommy:

exhausted

grouchy

serious

stern

responsible

reliable

preoccupied

dependable

I am the one who wants to just enjoy being your Mommy

watching you grow and change,

but I am Mommy, and I don't have that luxury!

A part of me wonders, "Am I good enough?"

Raising a child is serious business.
How do I do what's best, teach what's important,
guide along the right path,
without becoming the parent from Hell?

I am Mommy;
blessed and stressed,
wondering, "Am I good enough?"

FULL CIRCLE
(Dar Es Salaam, Tanzania)

As I stand at the ocean's lip,
with her spray kissing my face,
I pay homage to the many millions lost.
I give thanks for my spiritual return,
even in a different vessel,
Because I know that I am home.

I do not know my language,
but I am the legacy.
I do not know my name,
but I recognize my people
I do not know my original village,
but I know that I am home.

With a silent tongue,
I call out to the uncounted ancestors
who chose wet, salty graves;
the ones who fought until

their last breaths, but received no honor,
the fathers and husbands who killed
their families so they might die free;
the sons and daughters who arrived
on the shores of the Americas and LIVED,
suffering under history's longest human atrocity,
somehow holding on to the belief
That I would one day taste liberty.

Ancestors, I call out to you-
Your children have survived!
Mother Africa, embrace your daughter.
Hatujambo!
Mama Afrika, mkumbatie binti yako.
Najisikia nyumbani!

I have come home! I have come home!

CRASH

We met
at the intersection of Innocence and Ignorance,
at the crossroads of Loneliness and Entitlement.

My skin-hunger collided head on with your greed;
at the corner of Naiveté and Jock Status,
there was a wreck,
and it was me.

Shattered, dented, I arose from the rubble,
heading straight to the body shop
to be hammered out, sanded and painted
until I shone.
Extra large seat covers hid the torn upholstery of my spirit;
new mirrors deflected the pain in my eyes,
but if you checked CARFAX
you would have found my true history:

Pretty and new, fresh off the lot,
I zipped along the youthful highway,
ignoring the big yellow SLOW DOWN
and sliding right through STOP.
Perhaps I considered the speed limit
as a guide for minimum acceleration,
but certainly I did not YIELD.
And then I approached that BAD CURVE where we met.
The warning bells were silenced by the revving of my engine.
The flashing lights dimmed in the brightness of my high beams
and I CRASHED
directly into you.

At the intersection of Innocence and Ignorance,
at the crossroads of Loneliness and Entitlement,
there was a wreck,
and it was me.

SHEARLING

You've left me before you're even gone,
but still, your spirit is with me...always.

I need to do something
to ease the pain of losing you so suddenly

So I sing to you in your absence
Holding an old shearling coat
you stored in my closet,
planning to pick up when it got cold.
I sing "No One" to you for hours
in the dark of my house
before my altar.
I sing into your fleece collar
until I am hoarse/
but no one can hear

Yet, I believe you do

have to believe you do

I sing and I wail
WHY GOD, WHY?

My tears soak the leather of your coat,
releasing your scent locked into its pores
I wrap myself around it like it's you I am protecting,
though you always protected me,
and I sing,
breathing you into me deeply
where you can never be taken away
where cancer can't reach you
and you are always big and strong
my guardian

So I sing
and touch your whole garment.
The hem alone isn't enough

to hold or heal my grief
this is a song of loss and triumph too great
to be contained in one row of stitches
I let the entire coat touch me
and I touch it,
as if that winter coat could tell me
why God, why;
and I rock it and caress it like it's my baby
being lain in a cradle
because it has your essence all over it
your spirit is all in it
and I feel you when I put it on

Then I sing a lullaby
and hug your coat to me,
spread it over me,
to remember
how you covered me
when I was vulnerable,

how you carried me when I was broken
and broke me when I was too hard,
as I drift off to sleep
singing softly,
"No one..."

REDEFINING NORMAL

When the center of your world is gone,
with what do you fill the void?

When the foundation has been swept away,
upon what do you stand?

When the rhythm that set the timing of your pulse
has been silenced,
how can your heart beat again?

You have to redefine normal.

In that brief moment just between no longer asleep
but not fully awake,
you forget that life is forever changed.

As your feet feel the cold shock of the floor in the morning
you are reminded that

you will never walk with your beloved again,
but you still have to walk,

you will never again inhale the sweet scent
of her face powder mixed with Chanel No. 5,
or essential oils heated by his skin,
or the way peppermint floats from their lips,
but you still have to breathe.

You will never again sit down to
compose a grocery list,
go to the market on a Saturday morning,
come home and collaborate in the kitchen,
then enjoy the fruits of your labor- together-
but you still have to shop and cook and eat.
You have to redefine normal.

You can't just lie there in the comfort of
your flannel or satin sheets,

switching pillows every time one is soaked in your sorrow.

You can't just stay there and die too,
Although sometimes you think
that's what you want.
At some point you must arise
and return to the routines of life.

I didn't think my heart would continue beating,
but it has;
I thought I'd never want to laugh or dance again,
but I do.
I didn't think I could stand alone,
but I have.

No, it's not the same.
I'm not the same.
My entire world shifted,
but I am still alive in it

and I still have to do the "normal" things;

I just had to redefine normal.

WINTER SOLSTICE
(For Tray)

Last day of prolonged Night,
just before Sun started
to reassert her authority,
you transcended this earthly life.

Just when darkness became unbearable,
you became light.

Just when hours until dawn
seemed to slow nearly to agonizing halt,
you moved to Time Eternal.

Now I have new reason to
celebrate the year's shortest day,
not just because it signifies the promise
of longer days,
not just because it means
Spring will surely arrive,

but because it is the day when

you became an angel,

rose to your rightful place;

your work completed,

message delivered,

mission accomplished;

you joined the Source

of all illumination.

Shine, my friend, shine.

WHEN A BLACKMAN CALLS ME "BABY"

(For the BlackMen who love me...)

When a BlackMan calls me "Baby",

he speaks of an ancient understanding between us, saying:

Before the horror began,

I loved and knew you deeply.

When a BlackMan calls me "Baby",

a whisper leaves a distant,

but innately familiar shore,

travels across time and space

and accelerates as it skips atop ocean waves.

It becomes a Caribbean breeze,

drawing moisture when the palm trees

stir it into a gust.

Encircled, I sway in the vortex

of its wildly spinning wind, and I am

lifted-

above the mountains of worry and despair-
carried gently,
so gently,
back to the place
where our spirits first met:

When we were born into a culture that thrived for centuries
before we were even conceived

When we were children playing near the shore, calling out to
the waves that delivered our message to the horizon

When we lived in the safety of our village,
where men knew their place as fathers, leaders, protectors and
providers and women
were not ashamed to love and follow them.
Where wives worked side by side raising
each other's children and every child knew his father.

When a BlackMan calls me "Baby"
I hear that he remembers, deep in the fiber of his bones,
when our souls were mated by our common belief in the
gods/God of our ancestors

When, as kings, queens and emperors, we spoke to each other
in our own language.

When a woman was not under a man's foot, but by his side,
and a man was not a target for a woman's derision but for her
admiration and trust.

BlackMan, the way you call me "Baby" tells me that
if we reconnect with our deepest selves
we can return to that place where
our spirits first met,
before the horror began,
when we loved
and

knew

each other

deeply.

183 BAINBRIDGE STREET

I am from shoes and shoes and shoes and shoes!
that greet me at the door,
sometimes neatly 2 by 2,
sometimes, not quite.
I am from the brass hinge dangling on the wall,
the lone reminder of a door that used to hang there,
the door I sent flying with the force of my fall.

I am from the places where the gray paint
has worn away in the front yard,
from the wrought iron gate that needs
a new coat of shiny black,
from the newel post on the stoop
that moves if you nudge it.

I'm from the shadow of Most Holy Rosary School across
the street that gave birth to generations of scholars
but has now stood stoic and silent for a decade,

its steeple no longer watching over
James, Gail, Mariella y José
playing in the closed street at recess.

Yo soy de la bodega "Rodriguez" en la esquina:
"Una media libra de pavo, por favor.
Manny, es 'libra' the right palabra?"

I am from Callie who was Nana,
"Stand straight like a P not curved like an S."
I am from Wendi who was Lexi,
"Do what I say, Boo, not what I do."
Daisy who was Midgie,
"If your little friends in the street jump off
the Brooklyn Bridge, are you going to jump too?"
Nettie who was Net,
"God can do anything but fail,"
and Leon Edgar, "A luta continua" who was Pudgie and Moe,
and gave us short names

so no one else would shorten them.
I am from Johnny Ray,
"Straight talk means straight understanding," and
David Keith, "You don't have to go home,
but you have to get up outta here!"

I want to go back to peas and rice and curry
chicken that I don't have to make myself;
7-Up cake and candied yams from Nana's oven
Chicken fricassee, from Mommy's biggest, deepest pot...
I have her pot, but I just can't match her flavor.

I am from where I've been and where I am;
from the basement in my soul where that secret me lurks,
waiting to be summoned to the first floor of my life.
I am from where I've placed myself
and who I've chosen to become
I am from who I was and pray never to be again
I am Rhea Ummi Aloise Modeste, a work in progress.

05/31/2020:
A Haiku in Response to the Murders
of George Floyd and Breonna Taylor

Numb. Shield myself from

slow tumble into dark pit

Maybe can't claw out.

STORM

Just for the record, I always want you;
even when I am an angry hurricane,
my words flying at 150 mph, with tears
that could wash away a whole county.

Even when my cold winds seem to blow
strong enough to sever our bond,
as I rant and swear that I am cutting you off for good
"You didn't choose me; why do you come to me,
ringing my damn bell at 4:00 in the morning?"
I howl as my eyes become darkening clouds.

You're unavailable...you're not here when
I need you...you have too much baggage...
I know there must be someone out there who
loves me more than you do, who loves me first...

Each reason that I should leave you

is a brick in the levee I build
to hold back the flood of my emotions.

Then you come to me,
and bring the peaceful eye of my storm.
My cloudy eyes clear to reveal
a sun that rises especially for you.
My gales lose their force as if you were Jesus saying,
"Peace; be still."
My flood waters calm and recede,
lapping gently against the lifeboat of your arms around me
and I dismantle every row of bricks I used to shield
my heart against my desire for you.

Then the storm hits again, because it must, because it's real
and the peace I feel in its eye is only
temporary and stolen

But even when my clouds grow heavy and grey

and my gusts begin their destruction,
as the rain pours from me again in sheets
and the waves climb high against my levee,
even when I evacuate from myself
even then, I still always want you.

PASSION

Passion is the burst of color in the sky
as dawn brings respite from the gloom of a long night.
Passion is a tiger lily at the peak of its blooming
and a sea of psychedelic beach umbrellas viewed from the boardwalk;
orange, purple, yellow, fuchsia and chartreuse.

Passion is lightning interrupting a summer night sky,
promising rainy relief;
it's hot wings and curry and jalapeños and pepper sauce.

Passion is the rise and fall of the majestic Catskills
and watching intently the rhythm of a child
inhaling/exhaling/inhaling/exhaling.

Passion is throaty ballads and dancing in each other's breath;
it's Mardi Gras and Labor Day on Eastern Parkway.
It's the gentle brush of a mustache on a soft, sleeping cheek.

It's Saturday night AND Sunday morning.
Passion is reading poetry aloud.

Passion is my students' eyes, glued to the clock
in the last five minutes
of the last class
on the last day of school.

Passion is driving all night through the snow
to be there in the morning to say,
"Happy Birthday, Baby."

It's the last push to bring forth life;
it's reading 'til 2am to find out what happens;
the turbulence in the air before the first kiss.

Passion is gold and red,
violet and cobalt;
it's lifeblood, breathing,

silence and screaming.

Passion gives me energy to pursue what I love...

but when passion fades and all hope is lost,

it's my faith

that gives me the strength to open my eyes,

take the next breath, the next step,

to hold on until the next burst of color in the sky,

as dawn brings respite from

the gloom of a long night.

DREAMING A DECOLONIZED WORLD

I dream a world where applying for legal migration into the
U.S. is simple and clear,
especially for those seeking asylum and safety from violence
Where the pathway to this country is open and inexpensive,
not fraught with danger and exploitation
Where former Border Patrol Agents are multilingual Border
Crossing Facilitation Agents
who are trained to process
immigration applications fairly and expeditiously
Where Border Police Officers are there to keep
weary travelers safe from predators

I dream a world in which DHS stands for
Department of Hospitality and Safety
and ICE means International Cultural Exchange

Sueño un mundo dónde "la migra"
son las personas amable que se ayudan a través

del sistema de inmigración y a su hogar nueva

I dream a world where immigration detention centers are
repurposed as welcome centers to help new arrivals connect
with relatives, find jobs, and secure homes.
Where the cells are transformed into safe,
clean rooms in which families
can stay together while their paperwork is processed.
Where immigration lawyers, stationed at the welcome centers
with interpreters by their side to help people understand their
rights, charge the travelers nothing because they are paid by
the corporations that rake in millions of dollars in profits on
the backs of immigrants
Where there are classes for adults to start learning English
And mental health services for those who are suffering
But in my dream world, the suffering will not be caused by
the trip to, or the very act of crossing the border
I dream a world where "coyotes"
are only four-legged animals who sing in the night

and cartels are out of business

I dream a world where "border town"
means a place where newly arrived people
can easily find work and housing
Where there are schools that enroll children all year round
Where there are teachers who speak the children's languages
Where there are agencies to help
immigrants move on or plant roots.

I dream a world where a person que habla español and
walks into the United States at la frontera al sur
or someone who parle français
and drives across la frontière nord
or someone speaking English
who flies into JFK airport
will be treated with the same dignity and respect

I dream a world where the current

Immigration Industrial Complex
is dismantled and a new one is created that employs
thousands of people to help thousands of people
become productive members of the United States
to raise their families in peace and safety
to purchase homes and businesses
to then help thousands more after them

I dream a world where there are only
human beings, not "aliens"
and your very existence does not constitute a crime
just because your body has crossed an imaginary line.

I dream
Yo sueño
je rêve

HYPHENATED

"Mkosa milla ni mtumwa."
He who has no cultural identity is a slave.

I am

who I say I am;

am I not?

I am called African-American:

That strange hybrid species of human that has no homeland.

Africa/Barbados/Puerto Rico/USA:

That's the way my bloodlines flow.

Africans tell me distastefully that I am an Amer-i-can;

Caribbean Queens call me "Yankee Gyal";

In America, where I was born and raised,

I am just another nigger,

more privileged than some,

certainly blessed, but a nigger just the same.

On any street in Africa or the Caribbean,

I am "American", so extravagant, so arrogant.

On the street in America, where I was born and raised,

I am not seen as Teacher, Poet, Interpreter;
I am "thief", "welfare mom", "tramp".
In your mental dictionary, next to "American", do you see me?

In Anytown, USA, I am, at best,
outsider, interloper, novelty, or worse:
invisible.

In America, where I was born and raised,
I am fenced in, boxed out, red-lined and disenfranchised.
I am called African-American.
I ain't never called myself no kind of American,
'cause in the United States of Inbred Hate,
"American" don't apply to me.

I am who I say I am; am I not?
When George W. said, "My fellow Americans..."
he didn't mean me!
I am not African enough for my Continent-born

brothers and sisters;
And most white folks sure ain't claiming me in their America.
There is a ripple somewhere in the Atlantic that can tell me
who I am;
rusty chains rattle to tell my story, restless spirits whisper to
me in my sleep,
telling me to return to our Mother.
But Dear Mother, my siblings won't claim me as their own.

African-American.
I am both; I am neither.
I am the lost child of the Diaspora.
I am the wandering daughter of a distant mother.
The hyphen covers the part of me that is
missing.
I am who I say I am;
am I not?

HAIKU: WONDERING

My teachers said She

doesn't meet her potential

Am I still that kid?

WAILING WALL

I need me a wailing wall
A place to release my sorrows
those burdens that weigh heavily on my heart
I need me a wailing wall
A place where I can scream
until my throat is raw
and my heart is free
where I don't have to pretend
that I'm not hurting
that I'm "strong"
I need me a wailing wall
that I can lie beside
while my tears soak the earth it stands on
I need me a wailing wall
a place to store the pain
so it doesn't smother me
some place to rant and rail and vent
where no one will try to fix me

No, I am NOT ok.

I can put my face to my wailing wall

and tell God why I'm so mad

and my wall won't say,

"It's all in God's plan."

My wall won't say anything.

It will hold me up while I'm

flailing,

swaying,

rocking.

I need me a wailing wall.

HEY HIPS!

Broad enough to bring forth life- squirming, kicking and
announcing herself into the world-
without breaking
Hey Hips!
Strong enough to stand up again
after the cruel blow of grief
Real enough to publicly bear your pain
Hey Hips!
Your sway and flow disrupt
the onslaught of white supremacy
Your swing invites your sisters
to lock, and take up, arms together
Hey Hips!
Your hourglass knows the secrets of eternity
Your curves invoke ancient feminine energy
Your arc engenders joy and envy
Your rhythm is the primeval percussion of Mother's heartbeat

Hey Hips!

Wide to hold dignity

Solid to support roots

Round to inspire dreams

keep undulating

keep rolling

keep rocking and bumping

forward

upward

onward

to freedom

MY PEN IS MY SWORD

(For the youth of Lawrence, MA)

Don't tell yourself what you can't do

You have generations of precedents ahead of you.

A foolish teacher told Malcolm

what he could never be;

that brother sat down and read the whole dictionary!

Before he so prematurely left us,

he taught Black men they had to seek their own justice.

Bull Connor told Martin we would never be free and here you

sit, part of a King's legacy.

The law said if you were Black or Brown,

words you could not decipher,

yet Toni Morrison earned the Nobel in literature!

But it's not just the heroes of bygone days,

you have examples in your midst-

now follow their ways...

From the village of Williamsburg

two Boricua boys split

and earned more degrees than I got time to list.

Little Italian kid grew up in a Brooklyn tenement, playing
football to his heart's content.
Always loved the literature that he was taught, now look what
his passion has wrought.
Writing leaders from the "City of the Damned"- no,
the City of Promise —
they took their education in hand.
From LHS, Central Catholic and beyond,
they have been nurtured by the ABL bond.
We want the state receiver to acknowledge
every single one of them has graduated from college!
My pen is my sword, my voice is my shield.
I write, I speak, sometimes I cuss and cajole
'cause I need you to recognize that you're beautiful,
complete and whole.

My pen is my sword, my voice is my shield.
I write, I speak, sometimes I holler and swear 'cause I need
you writers to know

YOU are the only ones who determine

how far you can go.

FOR THE LAST RESPONDERS

They receive the zippered black bags the shrouded remains

of bus drivers

nurses

cops

sanitation workers

train operators

doctors

mothers

fathers

brothers

sisters

children

friends

not the frontline-

they are the last line

accustomed to giving a hug, holding a hand now they must

stand 6 feet away

in their somber suits

while one of us, alone, hovers over what used to be
what could have been
what will never be
They are not the first responders
no 7pm clapping or banging pots for them
They are the last responders
When all that could be done has been done
they come forward to receive what's left.

INHALE

Breathe

Just breathe

Never thought about it until I couldn't

Breathe

Twenty-one years old

Bereaved

Motherless child

Childless mother

Breathless

No more breath for my Mommy;

never any breath for my baby.

Then I understood

I had to breathe to live

I had to breathe to love

To bring forth new life,

first I had to inhale

Deeply and fully breathe

Deeply and fully love myself

Gasping for air taught me the value of breath

of life

of love

I had to nearly die to learn how to live

Just breathe

Just love

Just live

BLESSED AND HIGHLY FAVORED

I used to be afraid to speak my truth, afraid to be myself
but now I am courageous, free and vehemently me!
I used to think I was incomplete but now I know I am whole.
I used to believe my skin was not light enough
to be beautiful and not dark enough to be radiant,
my eyes not blue enough to evoke images of the ocean,
not black enough to be penetrating;
but now I know my skin is sweet mocha and my dark
brown eyes issue an invitation
to look intimately into my soul.
I used to have body image issues,
thought my hips too wide, legs too thick,
waist not small enough
but then I labored for 30 hours and pushed out life,
so now I know I'm BAAAD!
I used to let the world define me
but now I know who I am and whose I am:
a blessed and highly favored woman of God.

MY NANA WAS A MAGICIAN

My Nana was a magician and a culinary artist, too

Nana's house always smelled like something good cooking,

something sweet baking

She could take a cup of rice, a can of no-frills beans,

some leftover chicken and broccoli

PRESTO! turn them into a plate-licking delicacy

My Nana was a magician and an interior designer, too

Her flair was evident in every room

ABRACADABRA! when she got ready,

the entire decor was changed

Nana painted every room, reupholstered furtniture by hand,

made new knick-knacks

My Nana was a magician and a landscape artist, too

Nana's yard changed at her whim

For a while it was a Japanese garden

with a babbling brook and tiny bridge

I joyfully traversed that little overpass on my tippy-toes

in Nana's urban sanctuary

My Nana was a magician and a fashion designer, too
All of us girl cousins had matching outfits with our initials on the pockets, red, black and green crocheted berets like we were our own Black Panther Party
Nana sewed our blended family together with every stitch.
My Nana was a magician.
Her love was her magic wand.

DISPLACED

I don't live where I'm from
Where I'm from pushed me out with soaring rents for tiny
boxes in sky-high buildings blocking the sun
with outsiders who claimed to love the culture of
where I'm from doing their best to erase it
Where I'm from broke my heart and my spirit
Chewed me up on its exploitative teeth
and spit me out on blood-covered asphalt
Where I'm from made me fight for my sanity
and a little space
away from the developers ringing the bell with bags of cash
away from the shadows of luxury condos
away from the collective psychosis of the oppressed
Now I'm from
golden sunrise in my kitchen window
pink sunset bouncing off the walls in my purple bedroom

neighbors who smile and say, "Hey Ummi!"

as they share their cultures through food and stories
Now I'm from
corner store where they know what I'm buying
Superhero Sub shop where they start fixing
my order before I open my mouth
Now I'm from the sprawling Lincoln Park that I've
claimed as mine
where I can walk in my own rhythm at my own
pace beneath endless azure sky
smiling as the children of the Diaspora
laugh and play all around me
Where I live is not where I'm from but I have found
peace and freedom right here
where I live.

WITH WHOM WILL I TEACH THE CHILDREN?

(For Bertram Michael Hunter, 1958-2001
Teacher, Colleague, Brother)

I keep thinking I hear your voice in this place—
Not words, exactly, but the resonance
that is exclusively yours here.
I always know when you're around a corner or on the next flight of stairs,
Because I can hear your bass booming in conversation. It doesn't matter how quietly you think you're speaking,
I always know you're there...
But now you're not
And I miss you indescribably. The kids miss you, too; they ask for you every day.
Because you respect them
Because you challenge them
Because you listen to them
Because you won't take their nonsense.
I understand why you can't come back / shouldn't come back / mustn't come back...

But your empty chair, clean desk,
quiet phone make my heart ache.
With whom will I teach the children?
Grading the history tests made me cry. Everyone thought it
was because our students did so poorly.
It was that, too, but really, I was missing you.
Your humor
Your honor
Your power
Your integrity in the face of a system that totally lacks it
understanding why you can't come back / shouldn't come
back / mustn't come back...
But your empty chair, clean desk, quiet phone make
my heart ache.
With whom will I teach the children?
I miss you reading me, "Don't even try it, Miss Honey-One."
Encouraging me, "OK, Miss-get-her-Masters-go-right-back-to-
school-with-a-baby-to-take-care-of-and-gotta-get-all-A's!"
Teasing me, "G'head and work that second job, girl."

Again and again, the students say,
"I'm doing this because Bert told me to, that's why."
'Nuff said.
They quote you like World Book,
Wikipedia and their favorite rap artists.
They look to you for guidance and a reflection
of themselves.
They see you as hope for what they might become.
I understand why you can't come back /
shouldn't come back / mustn't come back...
But your empty chair, clean desk,
quiet phone make my heart ache.
I keep thinking I hear you calling me, "Ummi, is that you?"

IF YOU ARE CAST ASIDE

Hold your head up

Receive your notice to vacate as a gift

Seek shelter where you are valued

First ask God to lead you

Head up

Notice to vacate? A gift!

Where valued, shelter

God first

A gift

Head up

God first

Gift

God first

Gift.

BECAUSE I KNEW

(for Adunni)

Climbing into your top bunk,
I held your little hand until your grip softened in mine.
Placing it gently under your covers,
I kissed your forehead and turned out the lamp,
because I knew.
I played silly games with you as we
walked along the busy streets,
leading you with your eyes closed,
swinging our arms back and forth,
running to make you catch me
and, with Daddy,
lifting your arms up high
as you squealed, "Swing me! Swing me!" at every curb,
because we knew
I read to you every night
even when I was so tired that the words
became gibberish, because I knew
Sometimes I changed my plans just to be with you or came

home early because you were unhappy.
I let you sleep in my bed,
despite criticism from family and media,
your exhalations tickling my cheek,
immediately aware if your breathing changed,
or your temperature spiked
or you had a bad dream,
because I knew.
I knew the day would come
when you'd go upstairs to bed, forgetting to say good night,
when holding my hand in the street or sharing a laugh with
me would be unthinkable to you
when the pleasure
of reading a story with me
would pale in comparison to playing games on your laptop
when you would be happy to see me go out,
leaving you home and free of my scrutiny
I knew this day would come,
that you would grow up and away from me.

I've read it's the natural progression of time.
So I call you on your cell phone
when you've forgotten to say good night;
walk beside you, but not too close, in public
I pick up the books you like and read them to myself at night
when you're not looking
I enjoy the freedom your independence gives me while
I hush the quiet voice of fear and guilt
Watching you grow into the young woman
God intended you to be,
I celebrate the memories of the little girl you were.
And I give thanks for
every time I held your little hand in mine
every tear I wiped from your cheek
every schedule I changed and rearranged for your comfort
every night I stayed up late to do your hair
every story I read with one eye closed
because I knew.

About the Author

R. Ummi Modeste is proud to be both a native of Brooklyn, New York, and a graduate of the same NYC public school system in which she now teaches and guides students in their post-secondary planning. She is an alumna of LaGuardia High School for Music and the Arts, Performing Arts Division, Ithaca College, Hunter College and Empire State College of the State University of NY, where she has also served as an adjunct professor of educational studies.

In addition to her full-time job at City-As-School High School, Ummi is an active member of the Bread Loaf Teacher Network, an international group of teachers who strive to provide innovative and engaging ways for their students to become stronger readers and writers. Every summer, she is one of the facilitators of the Andover Bread Loaf Writing Workshop (ABL), a two-week professional development workshop held in Andover, MA that focuses on social justice work through literacy.

Ummi is the proud mom of her son Tarence and daughter Adunni. She is mom-in-love to Jean Marie and her favorite role is being Grammie to Nasir and Skyler.